The Tiny Book of Fashion

BOOK OF KATHERINE

ISBN: 979-8-9990512-1-9

Cover design by: Book of Katherine
Cover photo: Yulia Petrovskaya
Back cover photo: Amith Tiwari

In the beginning was the Word...
-John 1:1

Where would fashion be without literature?
-Diana Vreeland

CONTENTS

PART ONE

IN THE BEGINNING

CHAPTER ONE
THE LOOK

The Look. We all want it. But few find it.

I hope to solve that for you. You can find it. I promise. So listen and listen well.

The Look cannot be found in one place. It is found in many places, high and low, across the world. And it is your job, in fashion, to find it.

But it's easier said than done.

CHAPTER TWO
THE LIE

"I was always fascinated by the absurdities and luxuries and the snobbism of the world that fashion magazines showed." -Diana Vreeland

You will be told what The Look is. Influencers, celebrities, fashionistas and mega-brands spend countless hours and endless amounts of cash to make you believe in *their* Look for *their* benefit. But that's not fashion. It never is. It never was. It never will be.

Throw that lie in the trash.

You will never find The Look in their book.

CHAPTER THREE
THE TRUTH

"Truth is a hell of a big point with me."
-Diana Vreeland

The truth hurts, but if you love fashion you'll die for fashion, so hurting a bit shouldn't be a problem, right? Right.

The truth is, you need to know yourself first. If you don't, you'll always walk, talk and wear a terrible carbon copy of somebody *else's* Look. And guess what? If you don't have your own Look, you will never, ever, *ever* be able to determine another's.

If you haven't found The Look, do us all a favor and don't work in fashion.

CHAPTER FOUR
THE BASIC FOUR

"The only real elegance is in the mind;
if you've got that, the rest really comes from it."
-Diana Vreeland

The Look goes beyond fabric and design. True fashion, at its core, has four core elements:

1) Who You Are
2) What You Wear
3) How You Walk
4) How You Talk

In other words:

Think –Talk – Wear – Walk.

That's fashion.

What you think, say, wear and do determines your fashion, nothing else. If you want to be good at fashion, you need to have your own point of view in more than just clothing and accessories.

CHAPTER FIVE

TO BE OR NOT TO BE
AUTHENTIC

"Style—all who have it share one thing: originality."
-Diana Vreeland

If what you think can be found on a t-shirt, bumper sticker, meme or headline, you are more than likely a non-playing character (NPC) in life. And it is impossible for an NPC to be fashionable.

Humans are complicated. We are totally different from one another. Learn how you differ from others, and you will learn a bit about yourself and grow much closer to your goal of gaining The Look and being fashionable.

Separating from the hive is difficult at first. The hive will not like it. But when you distance yourself enough – when you become more authentic than not – the hive will start to try and emulate you.

When that happens, you will have achieved The Look.

PART TWO

YOU

CHAPTER SIX
BE INSPIRED

*"There's only one thing in life, and that's
the continual renewal of inspiration."*
-Diana Vreeland

Fashion is the art of creation. And nobody creates without being inspired. Sometimes the wave hits you out of nowhere. Sometimes it flows in like the tide, slow and steady, until — *wham!* — you are ready to create.

But only the best know how to constantly create, which is what fashion requires. Only the best know how to cultivate inspiration. Only the best know the secret behind inspiration.

Until now.

CHAPTER SEVEN
DELIGHT AND SURPRISE

"If it isn't a passion, it isn't burning, it isn't on fire, you haven't lived." -Diana Vreeland

Walk into a vintage store. Ignore the sizes. This isn't about finding your size. Ignore the gender. This isn't about finding what you can wear. This is about being inspired. And you need to start by finding pieces that delight, fascinate or surprise you.

Start by looking around the store's racks of clothing, shoes and accessories and pick one. And pick that first rack *carefully*.

Which rack has the most life? Looks the most complicated? Has the kind of colors that make you feel good? Don't pick a rack based on what you normally buy.

This exercise is not about buying. Inspiration is never about buying. This exercise is about you — waking up that part of you that *generates* — that *invents* — that *creates*.

We are made in the image of God. And God is Creation itself.

It's time to wake up the creator in you. So pick a rack that feels exciting. And then? Walk towards it.

CHAPTER EIGHT
FEAR NOT

"Beauty is in all beings that love and are loved."
-Diana Vreeland

Look at every item on the rack. Decide which piece excites, puzzles or fascinates you the most. And then take that item only off the rack for a closer look.

And then spend some time admiring it.

Think.

Ask yourself: Why? Why do I like this piece? How does it make me feel? Why? Is it the fabric? The color? The patterns? The cut? The stitching? The shape? The functionality? The design? All of it together? Or is it just the spirit of the item as a whole?

True fashion is rooted in what moves us deep in our souls. And you need to know what moves you. But more importantly, you need to know *why*. No one can do this for you. You must do it for yourself.

And then, put the item back. And move on to the next rack and repeat the process. Not every rack will have an item that inspires you. And even less will have more than one item that does.

I once came across a small vintage store in New York where I could write a paper on every single item on a single rack. To this day, I am convinced that I walked through a magic portal. I've never seen it before. I've never seen it since.

Don't be surprised if you walk out of a storefront having only been inspired once or twice. Be grateful. Most go through life uninspired for years at a time. And they don't know fashion.

CHAPTER NINE
INSIDE AND OUT

"Fashion must be the most intoxicating release from the banality of the world." -Diana Vreeland

Over time you will grow. You will become picky about what inspires you. Learn to rate how much something delights or titillates you on a scale of 1-10. Do not be afraid to enter a museum and study everything in it, only to realize that you think it's all junk. The tree outside holds more inspiration in a single leaf.

That's okay. That's you. You didn't curate the museum.

The point is to know what you like, what you don't like and *why*.

But to get there, you must learn to sort through pieces one by one - the way you did in that vintage store — but in many, many, many other places. If done correctly, one can be inspired by a single rock in a gravel driveway, a single flower in a gas station garden, a single belt in a discount store and a single gem in three-story jewelry store.

Well, hopefully a three-story jewelry store will have more than one piece of inspiration for you. But you get my point.

Someone skilled at inspiration will find it indoors and outdoors, in the micro and macro, in the dark and in the light. And when you've done this – when you've discovered the joy of being inspired, the stage is set for you to create The Look – for both you and others.

For to know what inspires you, to know what makes the generator in you come alive and create, is to truly know yourself.

CHAPTER 10
OWNING IT

*"When I arrived in America, I had these
very dark red nails which some people objected to,
but then some people object to absolutely everything."*
-Diana Vreeland

It doesn't matter what you think. It doesn't
matter what side of an issue you take. It doesn't
matter if the world seems inspired by a piece of
art that makes you yawn. It doesn't matter if a
single marble in a jar full of them happens to
tickle your fancy and delight when everyone
else says marbles are a thing of the past.

It doesn't matter what the world thinks,
feels, expects and demands when it comes to
what you wear. Because if you simply do what
they say, you will look awkward. You will look
like a downgraded version of an Instagram
post. You will look *less than.*

And fashion is about looking like yourself – not more, not less. And you are insanely loveable, loved and unique. No one has your Look. No one. Just you.

When you are ready to buy, buy something that excites you. And then make it stand-out by creating a background canvas when you wear it.

I'd suggest starting with an accessory that inspires and delights you, such as a pair of sunglasses, a pair of shoes, a single scarf or a handbag. Pick a complimentary color (black or white is always safe, but you can experiment with blues if your beloved item is orange or red, browns if your delightful piece is gold or green, etc.) and wear it head to toe. This way your item will stand out against a beautiful frame that you've created.

And you'll know it. When you walk and when you talk, you'll shine, because a piece that thrills you is visible, and it will feel like *you* are visible.

And that's the game.

Try it.

I promise, you will grow from there. This is just the start!

EPILOGUE
LAST WORDS

Fear is the enemy of fashion. We live in a society so saturated in media marketing that deviating from the norm feels like defection. But that road leads to antidepressants and self-destructive behavior.

Bad fashion is not a small issue. We live in a world that allows us to customize our music, our devices, our homes and our hair but not our fashion. Oh, no. Our fashion must align with the current trends. And that, my friends, is the recipe for a wasteland of *no-fashion-what-so-ever.*

I'd rather have fashion, no matter what the cost. And that requires the breaking of a few rules. That requires more than a few trendsetters. And I'm okay with that.

I'd rather be a trendsetter. I think you would too.

For that's what happens when we express our authentic selves to the outer world: we inspire others to do the same.

I once wore red lipstick into a fabric store, and an elderly woman looked up at me and said, "I wish I could wear red lipstick."

She broke my heart that day. There are so many different shades of red in so many different formulas today that everyone can enjoy looking fantastic in a red lip. The right red lipstick shade brings out the life in our cheeks and gives us a healthy glow. Why should anyone *fear* wearing red lipstick!?

But she lived in an area of the United States where red lipstick is still considered scandalous.

As you can imagine, its streets are dreary, dull and lifeless. But I wore the red lipstick anyway. It was more important for me to be authentic, for death lies in the other direction.

I choose life. And fashion is a reflection of life.

Well, *good* fashion is life.

I invite you to join me in the adventure.

ACKNOWLEDGEMENTS
GRATITUDE & THANKS

This book is the result of my friends, fans and Diana Vreeland. My friends have kept me alive through fashion. My readership has been loyal in ways only family can be. They are my closest partners in crime. And Diana?

Diana Vreeland set me free.

I'll never forget the day I discovered her. With every turn of the page and every slide of the finger, I breathed a deeper and deeper sigh of relief. For the first time, I did not feel alone in fashion, and as such, the world. A voice like mine had come before. And I somehow felt both validated and whole all at once. I remember whispering that silent prayer: *Thank you, God.* And my life was never the same after that.

As such, I've decided to do things a bit backwards. I've already written this book. But tonight, when I decided to dedicate it to Diana with a quote of hers to start it off, I found the task impossible.

Diana had already read my mind – long before I was born. So I am giving up and adding a quote of hers to each chapter. I think that's only fitting, don't you?

Alas, I studied Shakespeare instead of Vreeland in school, but I am convinced that the world I grew up in was shaped by her in ways untold. She made it possible for me to find myself by influencing the world I was born into. (Thank you, Vogue, for catapulting her to the heaven she deserved.)

And finally, this book would not be possible if I did not bend my knee to one and only one. From him my life flows – and I yearn to flow for him – forever. (IFYKYK.)

Now. Let's fashion.